BFF

A KEEPSAKE JOURNAL OF Q & As FOR Best Friends

LAURA BARCELLA

STERLING CHILDREN'S BOOKS
New York

STERLING CHILDREN'S BOOKS
New York

An Imprint of Sterling Publishing
387 Park Avenue South
New York, NY 10016

Interior illustrations by Ellen Duda
Cover illustration by Bethany Robertson
Cover design by Merideth Harte

ISBN 978-1-4549-1396-2

Distributed in Canada by Sterling Publishing
c/o Canadian Manda Group, 165 Dufferin Street
Toronto, Ontario, Canada M6K 3H6
Distributed in the United Kingdom by GMC Distribution Services
Castle Place, 166 High Street, Lewes, East Sussex, England BN7 1XU
Distributed in Australia by Capricorn Link (Australia) Pty. Ltd.
P.O. Box 704, Windsor, NSW 2756, Australia

For information about custom editions, special sales,
and premium and corporate purchases, please contact
Sterling Special Sales at 800-805-5489
or specialsales@sterlingpublishing.com.

Manufactured in China

Lot #:

2 4 6 8 10 9 7 5 3 1

10/14

www.sterlingpublishing.com/kids

Oh, hello there!

This book you're holding in your hands is a special journal made just for best friends to complete together! That's right—it's a diary for BFFs. How fun is that? This journal is practically overflowing with quizzes, questions, prompts, and places for you to wax poetic about all the great (and less-than-great) things that make up your crazy lives. Of course, it also features questions about your oh-so-important relationship with your best friend, because really, what's life without a bestie to share clothes, food, friends, and stories with?

From "would you rather" games to multiple-choice quizzes to lists of your favorite things, less than favorite things, and everything in between, *BFF* will help you both reflect on your lives. When you've finished, tuck this book away so that when you pick it up in ten or twenty years, you'll have a super-specific look at one of your most meaningful friendships, not to mention a window into who you were when you were younger.

Throughout this book you'll notice that each activity has two areas to write or draw on. Before you begin, each of you claim a color—either **pink** or **teal**—and then throughout the book, stick to your colored area as you're completing the activities. Write your names here on your chosen color:

_____ _____

Now get cracking—go forth and journal!

Stare at your best friend for three minutes straight. Time it! Then draw sketches of each other's faces.

Be sure to capture whatever strikes you as the most unique or interesting features of your friend's face!

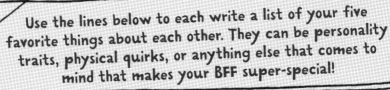

Use the lines below to each write a list of your five favorite things about each other. They can be personality traits, physical quirks, or anything else that comes to mind that makes your BFF super-special!

1. _____

2. _____

3. _____

4. _____

5. _____

1. _____

2. _____

3. _____

4. _____

5. _____

Make up a playlist for your best friend's **rockin' birthday bash**. What five songs would NEED to be played? Feel free to include YOUR favorites as well!

_____   _____

_____   _____

_____   _____

_____   _____

_____   _____

Write the outline of a short story.

The only rule is that your story must feature your best friend as the hero or heroine who totally saves the day!

_____
_____
_____
_____
_____
_____
_____
_____
_____
_____
_____
_____
_____
_____

If you could give yourself a **style makeover**, what kinds of clothes would you most like to start wearing? (For example, what brand of shoes would you die to snag a pair of? Or what style of dresses would you most want to wear?)

We know you love a good movie. Who doesn't, right? Go ahead and write a list of your five absolute all-time **favorite movies** EVER below!

_____   _____

_____   _____

_____   _____

_____   _____

_____   _____

Imagine you and your BFF get stuck on
a desert island.

Use the space on these pages to each doodle the five things you'd most want to have with you.

Write down the five cutest things you've
ever seen your crush wear!
Maybe it's a cute pair of checkered
Vans sneakers, a black fedora, or
a cool pair of worn jeans.

_____

_____

_____

_____

_____

_____

_____

_____

_____

Would you rather not speak to your best friend for two years **OR** show up at school wearing only underpants?

_____

_____

Would you rather sleep in the icy tundra **OR** on a raft in the open ocean?

_____

_____

Grossness alert! Would you rather lick the bottom of your BFF's feet **OR** eat all the clumps out of a cat's litter box?

_____

_____

On this page and the next, you and your BFF fill in the blanks. Then compare your answers!

My favorite **holiday** is _____

because I'm **obsessed** with _____

and absolutely **can't stand** _____.

My current **BFF** is _____

and _____

is **special** to me because _____

_____.

When I think about _____,

I feel **butterflies** in my stomach because of

_____'s

_____, _____,

and _____.

My favorite **holiday** is _____

because I'm **obsessed** with _____

and absolutely **can't stand** _____.

My current **BFF** is _____

and _____

is **special** to me because _____

_____.

When I think about _____,

I feel **butterflies** in my stomach because of

_____'s

_____, _____,

and _____.

Put on your thinking cap and try to go back in time . . .
What's the worst thing that's ever happened to you?

_____

_____

_____

_____

_____

_____

_____

_____

_____

_____

_____

_____

_____

Write a paragraph about it and make a point to include at least one thing you learned from the experience.

Here's an activity for best friends to do together. Go outside and search for the **coolest-looking rocks** or stones you can find. Then bring them inside and paint them as a **fun little gift** for each other! Describe the rocks you found and how you painted them below.

_____

_____

_____

_____

_____

_____

_____

_____

_____

_____

Answer the questions below about your best friend. Write the answer that fits your buddy best.

From the list below, choose what your BFF's spirit animal would be! A spirit animal is the animal that's most like a person—a sort of physical animal representation of who they are.

An owl

A lamb

A cat

An elephant

_____   _____

From the list below, choose what kind of profession you can most imagine your BFF having one day.

Doctor

Artist

Teacher

Rocket scientist

_____   _____

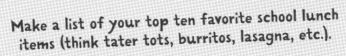

Make a list of your top ten favorite school lunch items (think tater tots, burritos, lasagna, etc.).

1. _____   1. _____

2. _____   2. _____

3. _____   3. _____

4. _____   4. _____

5. _____   5. _____

6. _____   6. _____

7. _____   7. _____

8. _____   8. _____

9. _____   9. _____

10. _____   10. _____

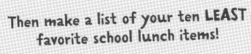

Then make a list of your ten **LEAST** favorite school lunch items!

1. _____   1. _____

2. _____   2. _____

3. _____   3. _____

4. _____   4. _____

5. _____   5. _____

6. _____   6. _____

7. _____   7. _____

8. _____   8. _____

9. _____   9. _____

10. _____   10. _____

Just for kicks, draw a little sketch of what you imagine you look like as soon as you roll out of bed in the morning!

Don't forget to include your crazy hair and/or
pillow marks on your face!

On the color-coded lines below, write out your **full names**, then use the **letters** in each name to write out as many words as possible! (For instance, in the name "Harry Edward Styles" there are smaller words to be found, like "always," "hardware," and "wrestler.")

_____

_____

_____

_____

_____

_____

_____

_____

_____

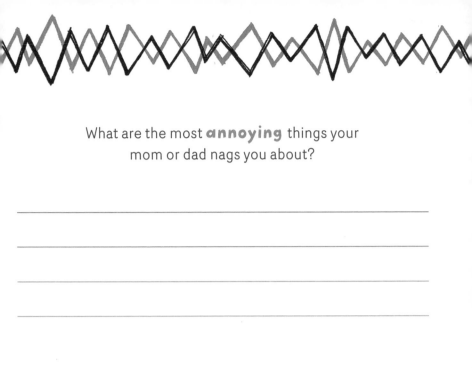

What are the most **annoying** things your
mom or dad nags you about?

_____

_____

_____

_____

What are the most **annoying** things your mom or dad
does when they think you're not looking?

_____

_____

_____

_____

What was your **worst fashion faux pas**? Write something you absolutely can't believe you left the house wearing.

Write down three fun things to do
during a snowstorm.

1. _____   1. _____
_____   _____

2. _____   2. _____
_____   _____

3. _____   3. _____
_____   _____

What's your very favorite only-in-the-winter activity?

_____

_____

Has your BFF ever had a crush on
someone you couldn't stand?
Write a few sentences about it here!

_____

_____

_____

_____

Have you ever had a crush on someone
your BFF hated? Who? What happened?

_____

_____

_____

_____

Would you rather get stuck inside an elevator for a week **OR** shave your head?

_____

_____

Would you rather permanently cut out the word "awesome" from your vocabulary **OR** permanently cut out the word "like"?

_____

_____

Would you rather be forced to drink nothing but rotten milk **OR** raw eggs for the rest of your life?

_____

_____

Be sure to include details about what you imagine your life will be like and what you hope to be doing.

Cut out your **favorite pics** of you and your BFF and paste them here and on the next page. Together, **decorate** the pictures, adding your own personal touches.

On this page and the next, you and your BFF fill in the blanks. Then compare your answers!

If I could travel back in time to another period in my life, I'd want to go back to age _____ because _____ was more fun then.

When I think about what my life will be like at age thirty, I imagine that I'll be living in _____ _____ with _____ and _____, and doing _____ as a profession.

The TV or movie character who most reminds me of myself is _____ in

_____.

If I could **travel back in time** to another period in

my life, I'd want to go back to **age** _____ because

_____ was more **fun** then.

When I think about what **my life** will be like at

age **thirty**, I imagine that I'll be living in

_____ with

_____ and

_____, and

doing _____

as a **profession**.

The **TV** or **movie character** who most

reminds me of myself is _____

_____ in _____

_____.

Imagine you and your BFF were getting cast in a new movie. What would the movie be about and what would your characters be like? Together, write out the details here!

Take a look at the questions about your BFF and write in the answer that fits your buddy best.

From the choices below, which do you think is your bestie's favorite holiday?

Christmas or Hanukkah

Thanksgiving

Halloween

Independence Day

_____ _____

Which of the slogans listed below could you most imagine your friend adopting as a personal motto?

Easy does it.

The early bird gets the worm.

Keep it simple.

All you need is love.

_____ _____

Make a list of all the **awesome animals** you've met throughout your life. It doesn't have to be a comprehensive list, just all the cool animals you can think of!

_____   _____

_____   _____

_____   _____

_____   _____

_____   _____

_____   _____

How many (or few) **animals would you want to have at home** if it were entirely up to you?

_____   _____

Organize a **clothing swap** with your best friend and a few other friends. Bring the stuff you don't wear anymore and shop one another's closets! After you've done the swap, use the space below to each write out a few of the great things you **traded** with friends.

_____

_____

_____

_____

_____

_____

_____

_____

_____

Write a list of five of the most embarrassing things your parents have said either **TO** you or **ABOUT** you in front of other people.

1. _____

2. _____

3. _____

4. _____

5. _____

1. _____

2. _____

3. _____

4. _____

5. _____

Write out one **secret** you've revealed to your
best friend only. (Don't worry—no one but you
and your BFF will see this journal!)

_____

_____

_____

_____

Have any of your friends ever revealed any of your
secrets to someone else via **nasty gossip**?
How did that make you feel?

_____

_____

_____

_____

_____

Use this page and the next to collaborate on a **collage** with your **bestie** using magazines, glitter, stickers, leaves, you name it!

Close your eyes, then draw one of your relatives' faces from memory!

Don't worry, it doesn't have to be perfect.
Be prepared to laugh!

Write out a list of five of your BFF's greatest secret talents (like tying a cherry stem in a knot with her tongue or singing embarrassingly awesome/awful karaoke).

1. _____

2. _____

3. _____

4. _____

5. _____

1. _____

2. _____

3. _____

4. _____

5. _____

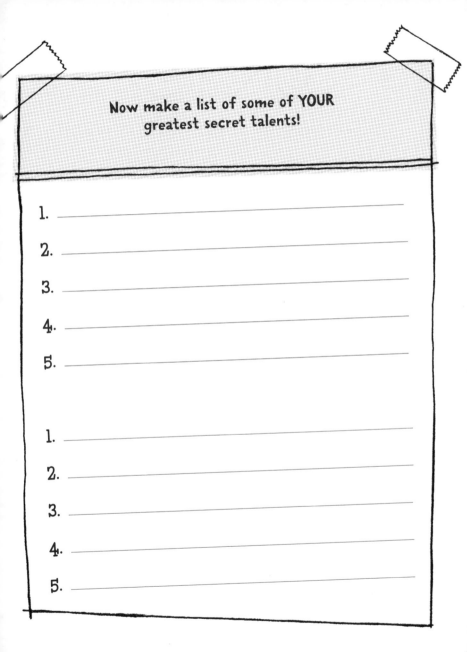

Now make a list of some of YOUR greatest secret talents!

1. _____
2. _____
3. _____
4. _____
5. _____

1. _____
2. _____
3. _____
4. _____
5. _____

What would your perfect mate look like?

_____

_____

_____

_____

What hobbies would your perfect
mate have?

_____

_____

_____

_____

What personality traits are most important for your love match to have?

_____

_____

_____

_____

What kinds of activities would you and your soul mate do together?

_____

_____

_____

_____

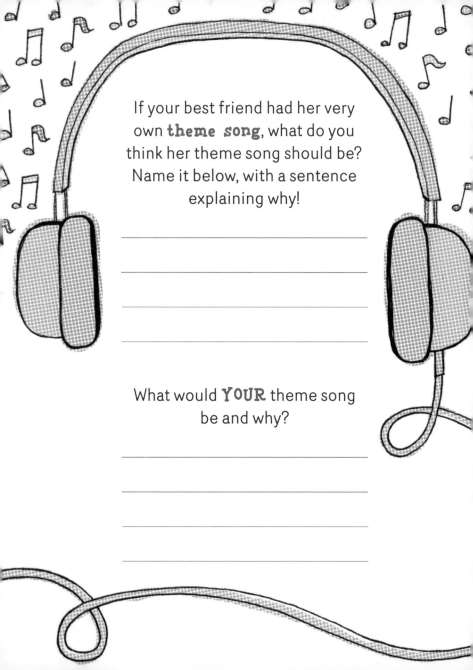

If your best friend had her very own **theme song**, what do you think her theme song should be? Name it below, with a sentence explaining why!

_____

_____

_____

_____

What would **YOUR** theme song be and why?

_____

_____

_____

_____

Imagine you developed a **superpower** allowing you to magically become **invisible** whenever you wanted to. What are some of the things you would do, places you'd go, and people you'd spy on with your newfound power?

_____

_____

_____

_____

_____

_____

_____

_____

_____

Of all the people you know in real life, whose **fashion sense** and **wardrobe** would you steal if you had the chance? Why?

_____

_____

_____

_____

_____

_____

_____

_____

_____

_____

List the five most annoying expressions you hope to never ever hear again. (For example, "amazeballs" or "YOLO!")

1. _____

2. _____

3. _____

4. _____

5. _____

1. _____

2. _____

3. _____

4. _____

5. _____

Would you rather lose your sense of hearing
OR your sense of smell?

_____

_____

Would you rather lose your eyesight
OR your hearing?

_____

_____

Would you rather have a constant weeklong case
of the sneezes **OR** the hiccups?

_____

_____

What was your BFF's biggest **fashion faux pas**?
Don't forget to draw it below!

_____

_____

_____

_____

On this page and the next, you and your BFF
fill in the blanks. Then compare your answers!

The **funniest** thing my BFF has ever said was

_____

_____

_____.

If I could pick my **last meal** on Earth, I'd pick

_____

_____

_____.

Rainy days make me feel _____

_____

The **funniest** thing my BFF has ever said was

_____

_____

_____.

If I could pick my **last meal** on Earth, I'd pick

_____

_____

_____.

Rainy days make me feel _____

_____

_____.

Make a **playlist** of songs that remind you of your **favorite movies**.

_____   _____

_____   _____

_____   _____

_____   _____

_____   _____

_____   _____

In general, what **genre of music** are you into the most?

_____   _____

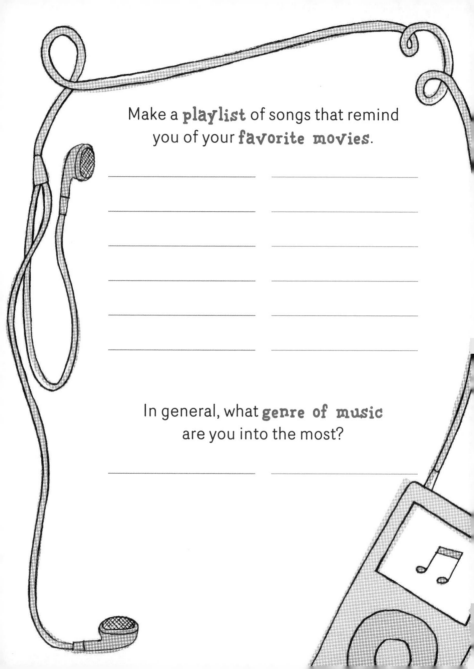

Together, think of the last **sleepover** you and your BFF had. Now write down all the details of your super-fun night below.

What did you **eat**?

What did you **watch**?

What did you **listen** to?

What did you **talk** about?

What time did you **fall asleep**?

What was your **favorite** part of the night?

Draw something related to your favorite sport or physical activity—without looking at the page!

Think outside the box! Yoga, skateboarding, and even walking count!

Write a paragraph (or more!) about the best day you ever had and what exactly made it so special.

What did you eat? What did you do? Who were you with?
Try to remember it in as much detail as possible!

Draw a picture of your very first pet, using whatever medium you choose.

(If you've never had a pet, draw your favorite animal!)

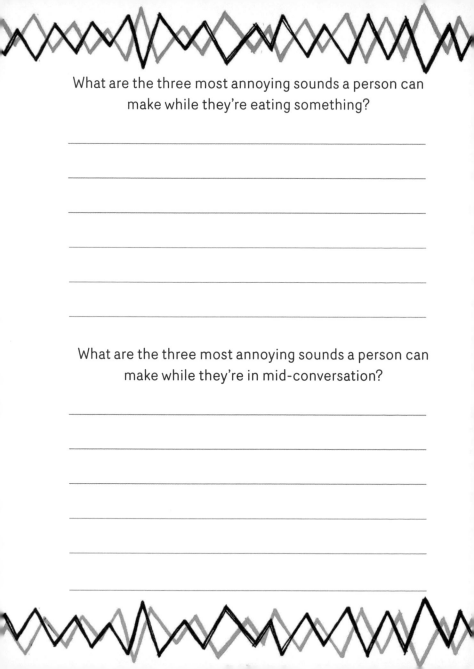

What are the three most annoying sounds a person can make while they're eating something?

_____

_____

_____

_____

_____

_____

What are the three most annoying sounds a person can make while they're in mid-conversation?

_____

_____

_____

_____

_____

_____

What's your favorite **healthy snack**?

_____

_____

What's your favorite healthy **meal**?

_____

_____

What's your favorite **UNHEALTHY snack**?

_____

_____

What's your favorite **unhealthy** meal?

_____

_____

Write "fan letters" to your favorite teachers of all time. Explain why you appreciate them and why you're such a big fan.

Use as many details as you can about
what makes them so special.

Write in the answers to the questions below.

From the list below, choose which animal other people are sometimes scared of but that you find harmless and nonthreatening.

Spider
Tiger
Dog
Snake

_____   _____

Choose which animal you find the most humanlike?

Cat
Dog
Rat
Dolphin

_____   _____

How would you describe your **personal sense of style** ... if you could only use five words?! Write them down below, then write down five words that sum up your bestie's style, too!

My style:

_____

_____

_____

_____

_____

My style:

_____

_____

_____

_____

_____

My BFF's style:

_____

_____

_____

_____

_____

My BFF's style:

_____

_____

_____

_____

_____

What's your very **favorite movie**? If you could rewrite the ending to it, how would you make it end?

_____

_____

_____

_____

_____

_____

_____

_____

_____

_____

_____

_____

List your top three celebrity
crushes below.

1. _____   1. _____

2. _____   2. _____

3. _____   3. _____

Now write down the three celebrities
you think would be a good love
match for your BFF!

1. _____   1. _____

2. _____   2. _____

3. _____   3. _____

If you could plan a trip around the world for you and your BFF, where would you want to go?

How would you want to travel (for example, plane, ship, car, train)? What would be on your itinerary? Write down all the details of your dream vacation!

What TV shows annoy you most?

_____

_____

What celebrities annoy you most?

_____

_____

What reality stars annoy you most?

_____

_____

Write in the answers to the questions below.

If you could pick from the list below, which of these TV shows would you most want your life to be like?

Nashville

Pretty Little Liars

The Bachelorette

Saved by the Bell

_____   _____

If you had to choose from the list below, which of these pop stars would you most consider a kindred spirit?

Lady Gaga

Rihanna

Carly Rae Jepsen

Nicki Minaj

_____   _____

Imagine that you're throwing a surprise birthday party for your BFF. Write out exactly what you'd do and what kinds of awesome things you'd plan, from the cake to the decorations to the invite list.

Write out a playlist for your **BFF's surprise party** (the one you planned in the last exercise). Be creative—this should be the BEST PARTY PLAYLIST EVER!

Would you rather eat chocolate **OR** vanilla ice cream?

_____

_____

Would you rather drink orange juice **OR** milk?

_____

_____

Would you rather eat pizza **OR** Chinese food?

_____

_____

Go outside during the next **sunny day** and look at the sky for a while. See how many **shapes** and **patterns** you can find in the clouds and then write them down below.

_____

_____

_____

_____

_____

_____

_____

_____

_____

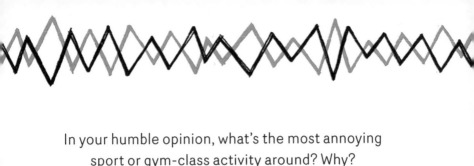

In your humble opinion, what's the most annoying
sport or gym-class activity around? Why?

_____

_____

_____

_____

What sport do you think gets a bad rap?

_____

_____

_____

_____

What's the **nicest thing** your best friend has ever said to you or done for you?

_____

_____

What's the nicest thing you've ever done **for your BFF**?

_____

_____

What's the nicest thing a **family member** has ever done for you?

_____

_____

What's the nicest thing **you've ever done** for a family member?

_____

_____

What's the nicest thing you've ever done for a **stranger**?

_____

_____

What's the nicest thing a stranger has ever done **for you**?

_____

_____

What was the happiest moment of your life?

What made it so special? What were you doing?
Who were you with? Write all about it.

Pretend you're bored in class and fill this whole page with random doodles. Go crazy! When you're both finished, compare your doodling styles.

Are your doodling styles similar or
totally different?

On this page and the next, you and your BFF fill in the blanks. Then compare your answers!

Getting up for school every morning is so

_____. I especially

_____ it when one

of my family members barges in to try to wake

me up! On weekends, my sleep schedule is

_____. I

_____ sleeping in.

My best friend is pretty _____

about getting up in the morning—it seems like

she wakes up a lot _____

than me.

Getting up for school every morning is so

_____. I especially

_____ it when one

of my **family members** barges in to try to wake

me up! On **weekends**, my sleep schedule is

_____. I

_____ sleeping in.

My **best friend** is pretty _____

about getting up in the morning—it seems

like she **wakes up** a lot _____

_____ than me.

Write in the answers to the questions below.

If I had to choose one chore from the list below that had to be done every day for the rest of my life, I'd pick:

Walking the dog
Taking out the trash
Scooping the litter box
Sweeping the kitchen

_____

_____

To me, the most irritating chore from the list below is:

Cleaning the bathroom
Making my bed
Scrubbing the toilet
Setting the table

_____

_____

Think of five **HILARIOUS** practical jokes you could play on your family or friends! **A** few suggestions: replacing the juice in the orange juice carton with prune juice or slipping a whoopee cushion on a classmate's chair.

1. _____

2. _____

3. _____

4. _____

5. _____

1. _____

2. _____

3. _____

4. _____

5. _____

What makes a person crushworthy to you? How does that differ from the kind of person your BFF crushes out on? Write about your preferences—and how they differ from your bestie's—below!

_____

_____

_____

_____

_____

_____

_____

_____

_____

_____

If you had to start wearing eyeglasses tomorrow, what would you want them to look like? Doodle a pic of your awesome new glasses here, then pass it to your friend to do the same!

Write out a playlist of songs you want to play at your next **birthday party**. Include songs that are upbeat and danceable, but also include slower songs and ballads to slow dance to. Romantic!

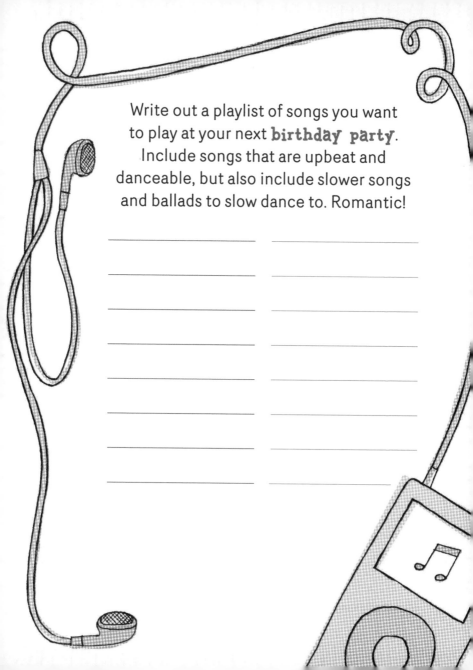

What are some of your **favorite smells** in the universe? For instance, cookies baking, fresh cut grass, the air after a thunderstorm . . . Use your imagination and write them out below!

_____

_____

_____

_____

_____

_____

_____

_____

_____

Would you rather eat duck **OR** eat lamb?

_____

_____

Would you rather never be able to eat sweets again
OR never be able to eat salty snacks again?

_____

_____

Would you rather live in a tiny town in the middle of
nowhere **OR** on an isolated tropical island?

_____

_____

Go outside for a walk together and see if you can find anything that would make a **good gift** for a friend or family member. For example: some wildflowers, a cool-looking rock that could become a paperweight, or some shells. Use your imaginations, then come inside and decorate this page with pictures of what you found.

Illustrate a scene from one of your most memorable dreams.

Try to remember all the details!

Have you ever seen a ghost? Write out the
scariest ghost story you can possibly imagine
(or one you've heard from a friend).

_____
_____
_____
_____
_____
_____
_____
_____
_____
_____
_____
_____
_____
_____
_____
_____
_____

Draw a picture of absolutely anything your heart desires. The catch is that you have to do it with your nondominant hand (that's the one you don't usually write with)!

Do your pictures look like what they're supposed to look like?

If you and your best friend could go on a double date with any two famous people in the entire world, who would you choose for both of you?

_____   _____

_____   _____

Why'd you pick those people? What do you think your date would be like?

_____

_____

_____

_____

_____

_____

Write in the answers to the questions below.

When it comes to aliens, I tend to believe that . . .

they're totally out there.

they're a figment of everyone's imagination.

I'm not totally sure what I believe.

aliens? What are aliens?

_____

_____

When it comes to angels, I tend to believe that . . .

they sooooo exist.

no way, I don't think so!

I'm on the fence.

I don't really care and this question is dumb.

_____

_____

On this page and the next, you and your BFF fill in the blanks. Then compare your answers!

In the scariest dream I've ever had, _____

_____ featured prominently. In the

nicest dream I've ever had, _____

_____ happened. Speaking

of dreams, I _____ remember them,

but not _____.

Do you have any recurring nightmares or bad dreams? What are they and how often do you have them?

_____

_____

_____

_____

In the scariest dream I've ever had, _____

_____ featured prominently. In the

nicest dream I've ever had, _____

_____ happened. Speaking

of dreams, I _____ remember

them, but not _____.

Do you have any recurring nightmares or
bad dreams? What are they and how often
do you have them?

_____

_____

_____

_____

If you could be in a **band**, what would your **name** be and what would you play? What role would your BFF have in the band? What kind of music would you make?

_____
_____
_____
_____
_____
_____
_____
_____
_____

What are your favorite ways to **relax** and **pamper yourself**? (Think bubble baths, naps, painting your nails, reading, drinking tea, eating popcorn—whatever works for you!)

_____

_____

_____

_____

If you could add one quick **pampering** act into each and every day, what would you add and why?

_____

_____

_____

_____

If you were a dog, what breed would you be? Do a quick silly sketch of yourself as a dog, then let your BFF do the same!

Woof!

Imagine you and your BFF were starring on a new **reality TV show**. What would the show be called and what would happen in the first episode? Together, write out some ideas below!

_____

_____

_____

_____

_____

_____

_____

_____

_____

Write in the answers to the questions below.

Which of these signs would you be most likely to make and hang on your bedroom door?

Keep Out! Yes, I Mean YOU!

I <3 Kittehs and Puppies Forevs

Welcome to the Queen's Lair

I'd Rather Be Dancing

_____

_____

If you had to give your life a number grade on how awesome it's been thus far, what grade from the choices below would you give it?

99 %

75 %

60 %

30 %

_____

_____

On this page and the next, make a list of five times you remember wishing you were somewhere else.

1. _____

_____

2. _____

_____

3. _____

_____

4. _____

_____

5. _____

_____

Some possible ideas: waiting at the dentist, getting a shot at the doctor's office, or getting a bad test grade back.

1. _____

_____

2. _____

_____

3. _____

_____

4. _____

_____

5. _____

_____

Would you rather be a famous ice skater
OR a famous skateboarder?

_____

_____

Would you rather hang out with Harry Potter
OR Lisa Simpson?

_____

_____

Would you rather be a mermaid **OR** a fairy?

_____

_____

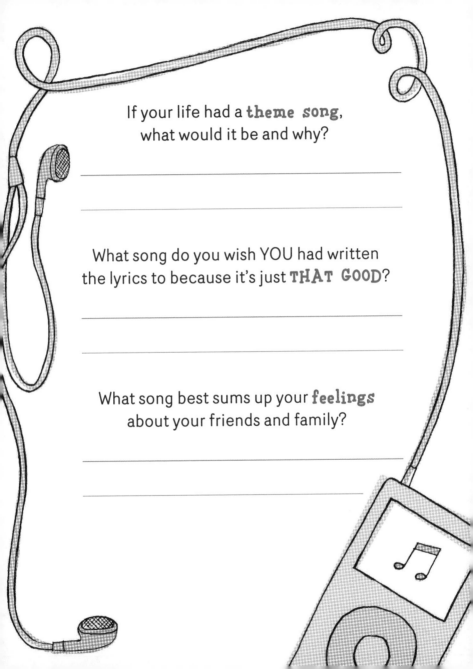

If your life had a **theme song**,
what would it be and why?

_____

_____

What song do you wish YOU had written
the lyrics to because it's just **THAT GOOD**?

_____

_____

What song best sums up your **feelings**
about your friends and family?

_____

_____

Think back and write out a list of the first names of ALL the people you've ever crushed on. Go way, way back!

My favorite soda is:

_____ _____

My favorite ice cream flavor is:

_____ _____

My favorite kind of cake is:

_____ _____

My favorite candy is:

_____ _____

My favorite kind of salty snack food is:

_____ _____

My favorite movie theater snack is:

_____ _____

Trace your hands on this page and the next.
Then adorn your sketched hands with pretty jewels,
rings, nail polish, etc.

You can even use real nail polish to color in the nails!

Write a few sentences about the three most embarrassing falls you've ever experienced. Have you ever oh-so-gracefully swan dived down the stairs in front of your school or slipped on the ice and face-planted into the snow in front of your crush??

1. _____

2. _____

3. _____

1. _____

2. _____

3. _____

Are you a **night owl** or do you like to go to bed **early**?

_____

_____

Do you usually **wake up early** or do you like to sleep in?

_____

_____

Do you ever enjoy an **afternoon nap** or do you think
naps are strictly for kids?

_____

_____

_____

_____

Remember when you were young enough to have your very own secret hideaway? Either draw it here or draw the hideaway of your dreams.

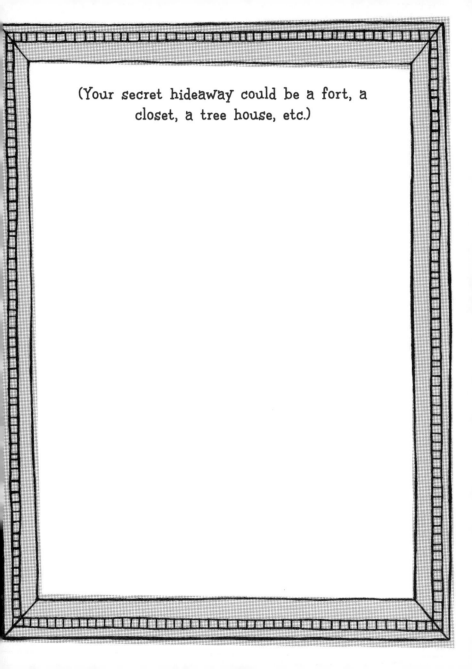

(Your secret hideaway could be a fort, a
closet, a tree house, etc.)

Together, create a **time capsule**. On separate pieces of paper, write down what each of you would say to your future selves. Then write down what you would say to the older version of your BFF. Put your letters in an envelope and tape it to this page to open in five years!

Make a list of the top five not-so-healthy foods you wish would magically transform into health foods. Go crazy! Donuts, chips, cookies, or whatever your heart desires.

1. _____

2. _____

3. _____

4. _____

5. _____

1. _____

2. _____

3. _____

4. _____

5. _____

Write out a playlist of songs you like to listen to when you're in a **bad mood**.

If you could hang out with only **ONE person** for the rest of your life, who would you pick and why?

_____

_____

If you guys could do only **ONE activity** together for the rest of your life, what would you want to do and why?

_____

_____

If you could travel to only **ONE place** for vacation for the rest of your life, where would you choose?

_____

_____

What was the most memorable first day of school you've ever had? What made it so special or memorable?

Write a little something about your most memorable first day of school and explain what exactly happened that fateful day.

On this page and the next, you and your BFF fill in the blanks. Then compare your answers!

When I grow up, I can totally see myself living in

_____. Hopefully I'll be

working as a _____, doing

_____ every single day. For fun

I'll probably _____ and I might

throw in a little _____, too.

The thing I'd LEAST want to be doing as a

grown-up is _____ because

_____ is incredibly

_____.

When I grow up, I can totally see myself living in

_____. Hopefully I'll be

working as a _____, doing

_____ every single day. For

fun I'll probably _____

and I might throw in a little _____

_____, too.

The thing I'd LEAST want to be doing as

a grown-up is _____

because _____ is

incredibly _____.

What are your favorite kinds of **animals**?
Write them down with at least one reason
why you dig each one so much.

_____

_____

_____

_____

What **qualities** or **traits** do these animals have
that you kinda wish YOU had, too?

_____

_____

_____

_____

What's the most annoying class you've ever
taken at school?

_____

_____

Who's the most annoying teacher you've ever had?

_____

_____

What was the most embarrassing time you were corrected or
yelled at by a teacher in class?

_____

_____

Quickly sketch the last three things you ate!

Which one was the yummiest?

Write in the answers to the questions below.

The season I love the most is:

Summer, duh

Winter isn't so bad, okay?

Spring!

Definitely fall

_____

_____

The season I most wish I could do away with forever is:

Fall—leaves are pretty, but so messy.

Winter—brrrrrrrrr, too cold.

Spring—flowers make me sneeze. Achoo!

Summer—too hot!

_____

_____

Imagine you and your BFF are traveling together on a ship that gets lost at sea. Make a list of the five must-have items that would help you guys survive.

1. _____
2. _____
3. _____
4. _____
5. _____

1. _____
2. _____
3. _____
4. _____
5. _____

Come up with an original idea for an iPhone app that
could help simplify or enhance your life.

What would the app do? What would you call it? Who would use it? How would it stand out from all the other apps out there?

_____

_____

_____

_____

_____

_____

_____

_____

_____

_____

_____

_____

_____

_____

_____

Imagine a **genie** suddenly materialized in the middle of your bedroom and told you she'd grant you **three wishes**, but there was a catch! The wishes could only be for your best friend! What three wishes would you choose to come true for your bestie?

How do you and your BFF compare when it comes to the **music you love**? Write a bit about how your musical taste differs (or is the same!).

_____
_____
_____
_____
_____
_____

Is there a certain song or artist that your **friend LOVES** that you totally can't stand?

_____
_____

Write a list of ten things you totally can't wait to do when you're a grown-up, like getting married, traveling the world, having an amazing career, or living on your own.

1. _____   1. _____

2. _____   2. _____

3. _____   3. _____

4. _____   4. _____

5. _____   5. _____

6. _____   6. _____

7. _____   7. _____

8. _____   8. _____

9. _____   9. _____

10. _____   10. _____

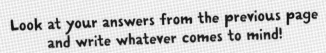

Look at your answers from the previous page and write whatever comes to mind!

Which of these things do you anticipate doing first and which do you think you'll probably end up doing last?

_____

_____

_____

_____

Which of these things are you most excited about?

_____

_____

_____

_____

Why not try a little **meditation**? Sit down on the floor with your legs crossed. Close your eyes and set a timer for three minutes (we're starting small!). Then sit quietly and count your breaths until the timer goes off. Don't worry about the thoughts that come into your head; ignore them for now and just focus on counting your **breaths**! After the timer goes off, write a sentence or two below about how you feel after meditating.

Think of a **fashion dare** for your BFF to try—for instance, wearing a headband as a bracelet, wearing her top inside out, or dressing in only one color from head to toe. Then have her write one down for you and discuss when you both can make your dares happen!

_____

_____

_____

_____

_____

_____

_____

_____

_____

_____

Would you rather show up at school wearing only clothes from your grandmother's closet **OR** from your dad's closet?

_____

_____

Would you rather never be able to eat candy **OR** never be able to eat pizza again?

_____

_____

Would you rather be allergic to chocolate **OR** salt?

_____

_____

Write in the answers to the questions below.

If I had to guesstimate, I'd say I spend about _____ hours on the Internet every day.

two

four or more

one

less than one

_____   _____

From the list below, my favorite social networking site is _____, hands down!

Instagram

Facebook

Tumblr

Twitter

_____   _____

On this page and the next, you and your BFF fill in the blanks. Then compare your answers!

The thing I like best about my **school** is that it's

totally _____.

That's not to say that everyone is nice, though.

_____ is kind of a **bully**,

and _____ is the **class**

clown. Most of my classmates seem to see me

as the _____.

I can't wait to be **done with school** this year so I

can _____

_____

_____.

The thing I like best about my **school** is that it's

totally _____.

That's not to say that everyone is nice, though.

_____ is kind of a **bully**,

and _____ is the **class**

clown. Most of my classmates seem to see

me as the _____.

I can't wait to be **done with school** this

year so I can _____

_____

_____

_____.

Write haikus to each other. **A** haiku is a three-line poem with five syllables on the first line, seven syllables on the middle line, and five syllables on the third line.

Write out a playlist of songs that
are perfect to listen to when you're
feeling great!

_____   _____

_____   _____

_____   _____

_____   _____

_____   _____

_____   _____

_____   _____

_____   _____

What **five qualities** do you find most irritating in a person? (For instance, you might hate when people act snobby, rude, or negative.)

_____   _____

_____   _____

_____   _____

_____   _____

_____   _____

What **five qualities** do other people seem to find generally annoying but that don't bother you that much?

_____   _____

_____   _____

_____   _____

_____   _____

_____   _____

What's the **grossest sandwich combination** you can come up with?

_____

_____

What's the **grossest kind of soda** you can think of?

_____

_____

What kind of **dessert** actually makes you want to gag?

_____

_____

Make a list of ten things you're totally obsessed with.

1. _____

2. _____

3. _____

4. _____

5. _____

6. _____

7. _____

8. _____

9. _____

10. _____

Things you are obsessed with can be anything, from hair products to pasta to colored pens.

1. _____

2. _____

3. _____

4. _____

5. _____

6. _____

7. _____

8. _____

9. _____

10. _____

Write a paragraph or more about a time when things turned out *completely* differently from what you'd been expecting.

What did you think would happen? What ended up happening? How did that make you feel? Did you learn anything from that experience?

Write down everything you and your
BFF **have in common**.

_____

_____

_____

_____

_____

_____

_____

_____

_____

_____

_____

_____

Now make a list of everything you
DON'T **have in common**!

_____

_____

_____

_____

_____

_____

_____

_____

_____

_____

_____

_____

_____

Are you **surprised** by how long either list is?

Make a drawing of one thing you're super afraid of.

Don't be scared!

On this page and the next, you and your BFF fill in the blanks. Then compare your answers!

If I could live inside any book, I'd choose to

live inside _____,

because _____

_____. If I could

live inside any movie, I'd want to try living

in _____ because

_____. The scariest

book world I could imagine living in is

_____, and the freakiest

movie world I could imagine living in is

_____.

If I could **live inside any book**, I'd choose to live

inside _____,

because _____

_____. If I could live

inside any **movie**, I'd want to try living in

_____ because

_____. The **scariest**

book world I could imagine living in is

_____, and the **freakiest**

movie world I could imagine living in is

_____.

Grab your backpacks and close your eyes.
Rifle around in your bags without looking
and pull out something random from the
bottom. Then sketch the random object.

Did you sketch similar items?

Write about all the variations on your name! First, write out **your full given name** (that is, the name on your birth certificate). Then write out the name your parents ALMOST gave you (ask them if you don't already know it!). After that, write out the name most people know you as. Finally, write out the **nickname** you WISH everyone would stop calling you!

_____

_____

_____

_____

_____

_____

_____

_____

If you and your BFF could be in a cover band that performed the songs of only ONE artist or **musician**, whom would you choose to cover and why?

_____

_____

_____

_____

What would you name your cover band?

_____

_____

_____

_____

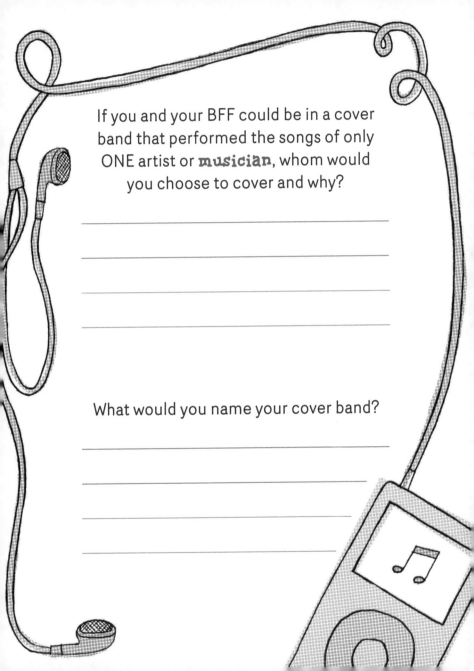

Who's your celebrity crush?

_____

_____

What makes your celeb crush so
special and crushworthy?

_____

_____

If you could meet your celebrity crush,
what do you think you would say?

_____

_____

_____

_____

Would you rather be forced to live outside in a Dumpster for a month **OR** in a creepy haunted house?

_____

_____

Would you rather be forced to drink a glass of dishwashing fluid **OR** rancid milk?

_____

_____

Would you rather eat a thrashing, live fish fresh from a lake **OR** drink a cup of cow's blood?

_____

_____

What are three of the **best vacations** you've ever been on, and what made them so incredibly all-around awesome?

_____

_____

_____

_____

_____

_____

What are **three dream vacations** you'd love to take one day?

_____

_____

_____

_____

_____

_____

Answer the questions below about your best friend.
Write the answer that fits your buddy best.

From the list below, which of the following things is your buddy most likely to NOT be doing this weekend?

Study. No way—not on weekends!

Go to a party—not into big groups.

Stay home watching TV . . . boring!

Play sports. No thanks!

_____

_____

If you guys were going out to dinner, which of the following kinds of cuisine would your BFF be most likely to go for?

Chinese, please.

Italian—you can never go wrong with Italian!

Indian—pass the curry.

Good old American!

_____

_____

Draw a picture of your dream house! The catch? It has to be a TREEHOUSE.

Make sure to include all the little details that would make your treehouse super special!!

What are three of the **goofiest fashion** trends that you actually—shhhh—kinda **secretly like** (even if you might not tell your friends that)? Time to come clean to your best bud! Write them below, with a couple sentences about why you like them!

_____

_____

_____

_____

_____

_____

_____

_____

_____

Make up a **new word** for a common illness or medical ailment. Choose a name that seems like it would fit the symptoms of the **condition** much better! For example, "nausea" could be "vomitoniculitis," and "cold" could become "sniffloenza."

_____

_____

_____

_____

_____

_____

_____

_____

_____

How do you feel about fairy tales?
Love 'em, hate 'em, take 'em or leave 'em?

Think of a fairy tale that has stuck with you and use these pages to revise it however you see fit. Bring it into the modern age and make it feel relevant to YOU, your BFF, and your lives.

What's the **meanest** thing you've ever done to someone?

_____

_____

How do you **feel** about what you did,
and did you ever apologize for it?

_____

_____

What, if anything, did you **learn** from that experience?

_____

_____

_____

_____

_____

Write out short snippets of conversation between you and one of your crushes. It can either be based on a real-life conversation you've had or it could be a discussion you dreamed up!

Again, try using your nondominant hand to doodle a picture. This time, do a quick sketch of what the outside of your house looks like.

This activity might be tricky, but it's not impossible!

Answer the questions below about your best friend.
Write the answer that fits your buddy best.

In twenty years, the city I could most imagine my BFF living in is:

Columbus, Ohio

New York, New York

Los Angeles, California

Savannah, Georgia

After high school, my bestie is most likely to:

See the world and learn about other cultures.

Go to college, obvs, then maybe grad school.

Work hard and make money.

Move somewhere super far away.

Would you rather have the word "fart-head" permanently tattooed on your forehead **OR** have your head shaved and never be able to grow your hair back?

_____

_____

Would you rather live in a house infested with tarantulas **OR** rats?

_____

_____

Would you rather encounter a vampire **OR** a werewolf?

_____

_____

On this page and the next, you and your BFF fill in the blanks. Then compare your answers!

_____ is my **favorite subject** in

school because _____

_____.

The **subject** I totally **CAN'T stand** is _____

_____ because _____

_____.

The worst part about being **my age** is _____

_____

_____.

The **BEST** part is _____

_____

_____!

_____ is my **favorite subject** in

school because _____

_____.

The **subject** I totally **CAN'T stand** is _____

_____ because _____

_____.

The worst part about being **my age** is _____

_____

_____.

The **BEST** part is _____

_____

_____!

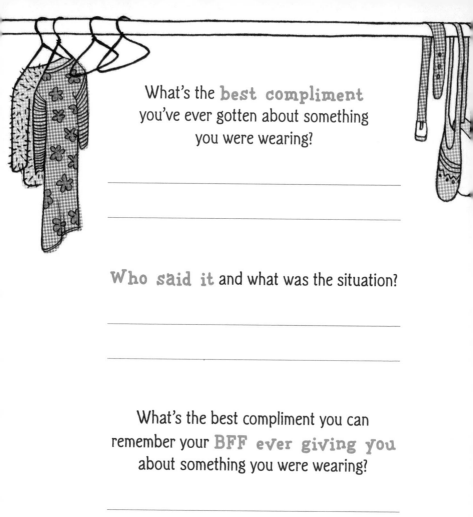

What's the **best compliment** you've ever gotten about something you were wearing?

_____

_____

Who said it and what was the situation?

_____

_____

What's the best compliment you can remember your **BFF ever giving you** about something you were wearing?

_____

_____

Make up your own rap song and write out all the lyrics below! And yes, your best friend has to make an appearance in it!

_____

_____

_____

_____

_____

_____

_____

_____

_____

_____

Think of five times you've felt really extra super proud of yourself and write a sentence or two about each instance.

1. _____
_____

2. _____
_____

3. _____
_____

4. _____
_____

5. _____
_____

Don't be shy—you totally rock!

1. _____

_____

2. _____

_____

3. _____

_____

4. _____

_____

5. _____

_____

What's the lamest **school trip** you've ever been on?

_____

_____

_____

_____

What **made it** so lame?

_____

_____

_____

_____

Describe it in a sentence below.

_____

_____

_____

_____

What's your **favorite milkshake flavor**?

_____

_____

_____

_____

Now make up your own **crazy** (but yummy-sounding) **milkshake flavors** and write them below. For example, would you ever think of making a cherry bacon cola or coconut orange fudge milkshake?!

_____

_____

_____

_____

_____

_____

Write a Valentine's Day love note to your crush. Feel free to say anything and everything you've ever wanted to tell them! This is for your and your BFF's eyes only.

_____

_____

_____

_____

_____

_____

_____

_____

_____

_____

_____

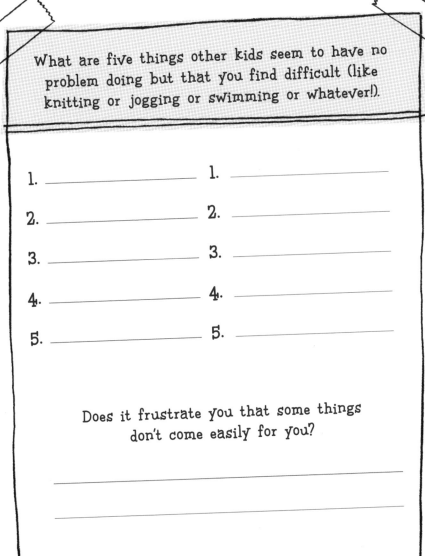

What are five things other kids seem to have no problem doing but that you find difficult (like knitting or jogging or swimming or whatever!).

1. _____   1. _____

2. _____   2. _____

3. _____   3. _____

4. _____   4. _____

5. _____   5. _____

Does it frustrate you that some things don't come easily for you?

_____

_____

Grab your **favorite** magazines and cut out pictures, symbols, and words that you think describe or represent your **friendship**. Paste them onto these pages. Feel free to further decorate your collage, or you can let the words and images speak for themselves!

Write in the answers to the questions below.

Choosing from the list below, the most crucial element of a perfect sleepover is:

Lots and lots of junk food

The right music to dance and spaz out to

Lack of parental supervision

Tons of scary movies

_____

_____

Of the options below, the most important aspect of a rockin' party is:

The music

The snacks

The people

The location

_____

_____

Write out a list of songs you'd put on a playlist that had the theme **"Huddled by the Fire in a Winter Wonderland."**

_____ _____

_____ _____

_____ _____

_____ _____

_____ _____

_____ _____

_____ _____

_____ _____

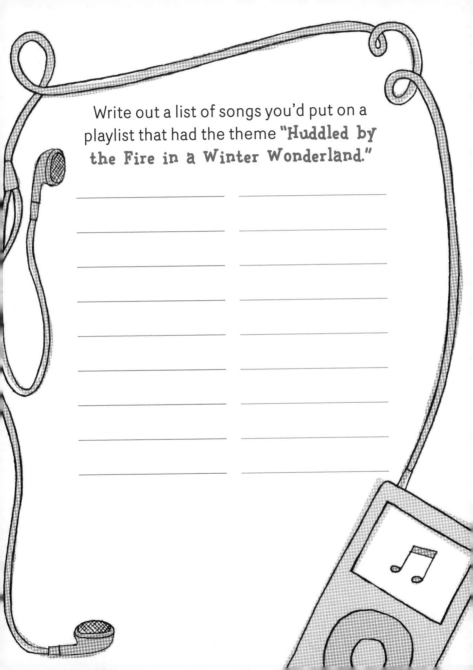

Would you rather never be allowed to get your driver's license **OR** never be allowed to move away from your hometown?

_____

_____

Would you rather be a famous actress **OR** a famous inventor?

_____

_____

Would you rather have to move to a new town with your family every year **OR** be stuck in the same place forever?

_____

_____

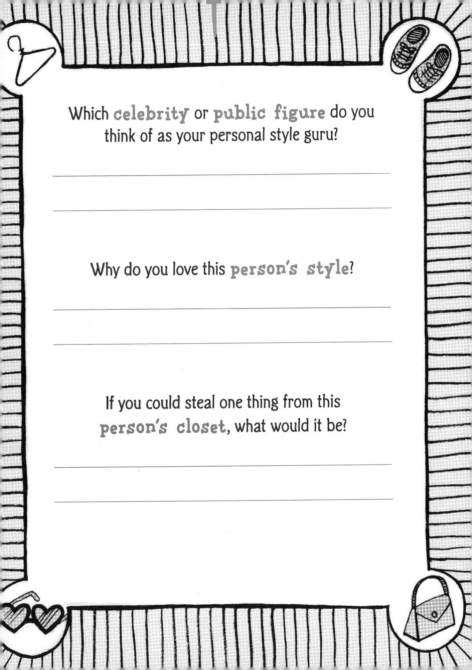

Which **celebrity** or **public figure** do you think of as your personal style guru?

_____

_____

Why do you love this **person's style**?

_____

_____

If you could steal one thing from this **person's closet**, what would it be?

_____

_____

Together, make a list of all the inside jokes you and your BFF have ever shared. Even the dumbest and grossest ones!

1. _____
_____

2. _____
_____

3. _____
_____

4. _____
_____

5. _____
_____

It's okay if you can't remember all of them,
just write down as many as you can.
(You'll love looking back at this in a few years!)

6. _____

_____

7. _____

_____

8. _____

_____

9. _____

_____

10. _____

_____

Imagine you and your bestie are given a **million dollars** to start your very own **business**. What would you want the business to be? What would your roles be? Write down your ideas separately below, then compare notes!

_____

_____

_____

_____

_____

_____

_____

_____

_____

_____

If you and your BFF could form a superhero duo, what kind of heroes would you each be? Together, decide what superpowers you would have. Don't forget to give yourselves cool names!

_____

_____

_____

_____

_____

_____

_____

_____

_____

_____

_____

_____

_____

_____

Quickly grab a pen, set a timer for three minutes, and doodle the first five things that come into your mind!

Did you guys doodle any of the same things?

What are some songs your **mom or dad loves** but you totally hate?

_____

_____

_____

_____

What about songs you **can't get enough** of but that your parents can't stand?

_____

_____

_____

_____

What are some of your **favorite smells**?
Write a short list and then let your BFF write some too!
These **scents** could be anything from perfumes
to fresh-cut grass to the smell of chocolate chip
cookies baking in the oven.

Now **compare lists**. Are you surprised by
anything your BFF wrote down?

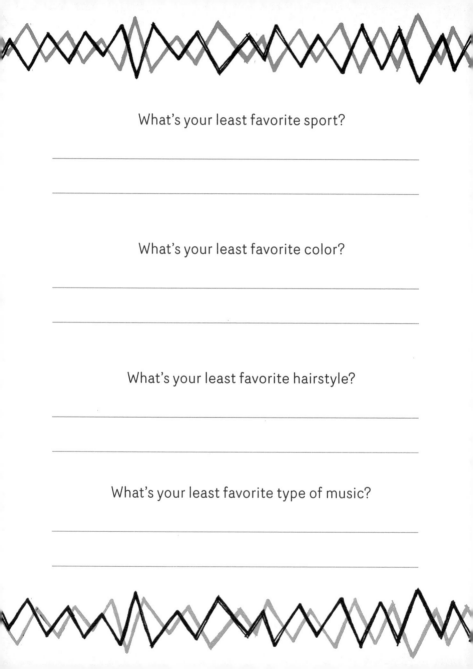

What's your least favorite sport?

_____

_____

What's your least favorite color?

_____

_____

What's your least favorite hairstyle?

_____

_____

What's your least favorite type of music?

_____

_____

Write in the answers to the questions below.

If you could visit any era from the list below, which historical period would you choose?

Medieval times—knights and queens, please.

Cavemen times! Let's go way, way back.

The Roaring Twenties (flappers, bobs, etc.)!

The 1960s for hippies, peace, and free love!

_____

_____

If you could go back and visit your mom during any phase of her life listed below, when would you want to visit her?

When she was just born, or soon after.

When she was a kid around my age.

When she was a teenager.

When she was fresh outta college.

_____

_____

On this page and the next, you and your BFF fill in the blanks. Then compare your answers!

My favorite **fast-food** joint is _____

because _____.

They make the most **delicious** _____.

When I go there, I usually order _____

to drink.

My favorite **local** restaurant is _____

_____. I've been **going there** since

I was _____. My **trusty** go-to dish there

is _____, but sometimes I'll get

the _____ instead.

My favorite **fast-food** joint is _____

because _____.

They make the most **delicious** _____.

When I go there, I usually order _____

to drink.

My favorite **local** restaurant is _____

_____. I've been **going there**

since I was _____. My **trusty** go-to

dish there is _____,

but sometimes I'll get the _____

_____ instead.

If you wrote an **autobiography** about your life thus far, what would you title it and why?

_____

_____

_____

_____

What **stories** about your life would you include in your autobiography?

_____

_____

_____

_____

_____

Would you rather wear a cooking pot on your head all day and pretend it was a hat **OR** wear a pair of tennis shoes on your hands all day and call them gloves?

_____

_____

Would you rather be forced to wear only the stuff that's in your closet for the rest of your life **OR** wear only athletic gear like sweatpants and basketball jerseys?

_____

_____

Would you rather wear the shoes you wore today for the rest of the year **OR** wear socks and sandals every single day?

_____

_____

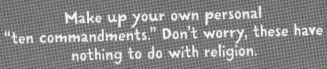

Make up your own personal "ten commandments." Don't worry, these have nothing to do with religion.

1. _____

2. _____

3. _____

4. _____

5. _____

6. _____

7. _____

8. _____

9. _____

10. _____

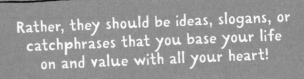

Rather, they should be ideas, slogans, or catchphrases that you base your life on and value with all your heart!

1. _____

2. _____

3. _____

4. _____

5. _____

6. _____

7. _____

8. _____

9. _____

10. _____

How do you feel about reality shows?

Which reality shows do you love, which do you loathe, and which do you hope to never see again (like, ever)?

What song instantly brings you back to a
different time and place in your life?

_____

_____

What song instantly makes you
think of a happy occasion?

_____

_____

What song instantly makes you
think of a **sad time** or a heartbreak?

_____

_____

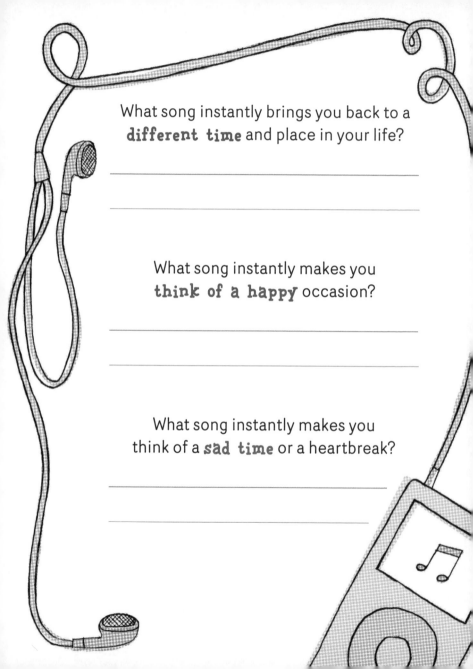

Do you believe in **astrology**?

_____

What is **your sign** and what does it say about you?

_____

_____

_____

_____

_____

Do you think the description of your BFF's
star sign seems **accurate**?

_____

_____

Choose an item of packaged food from the kitchen (for example, a box of tea, a carton of eggs, or a jug of milk).

Then draw or paint your item as faithfully
as you can!

If you were going to **start a blog**,
what kind would you start?

_____

_____

What would you name it and
what would you want to **write** about?

_____

_____

How do you **feel about blogs** in general?
Do you read many of them?

_____

_____

_____

_____

Think about some things you'd like to tweet at your crush if you could only work up the nerve. Draft a tweet below (you never have to send it, of course!). Remember, tweets are supposed to be 140 characters or less (including spaces!), so keep these short and sweet.

_____

_____

_____

_____

_____

_____

_____

Write in the answers to the questions below.

From the list below, choose which celeb is way overrated.

Hilary Duff

Rihanna

Britney Spears

Lucy Hale

_____ _____

From the list below, choose which celeb is someone to admire.

Lady Gaga

Taylor Swift

Selena Gomez

Kerry Washington

_____ _____

If you could be **best friends** with any character from a movie, which character would you pick and why?

_____

_____

If you could **DATE** any character from a movie, which one would you pick to date and why?

_____

_____

If you could have any character from any movie as your **sister or brother**, which one would you pick and why?

_____

_____

Create your very own series of emojis! (Emojis
are little cartoony-looking emoticons used in
text messages and in various phone apps.)

happy   excited   freaked out

sad   sleepy   sick

Draw one for each of the emotions listed,
then compare your emojis.

happy   excited   freaked out

sad   sleepy   sick

Milestone time! At what age do you hope to hit all these personal milestones? Write in your answers below!

First kiss:

_____

_____

First job:

_____

_____

First relationship:

_____

_____

First heartbreak:

_____

_____

First apartment:

_____

_____

Would you rather lose every single item of clothing you own **OR** never be able to change your shirt again?

_____

_____

Would you rather get chased by a dog **OR** chased by a giraffe?

_____

_____

Would you rather go on an exotic vacation in the African wilderness **OR** a snow-bunny vacation skiing in Colorado?

_____

You know how couples have **"their song,"** a song they love or have listened to together that has come to symbolize their relationship? What would your song be for you and your BFF? Name it, then **explain** your answer below!

_____

_____

_____

_____

_____

_____

_____

Write down all your favorite things to do at an **amusement park** (for example, play skee ball, eat cotton candy, ride roller coasters). You can even **rank them in order** from things you like to things you LOVE.

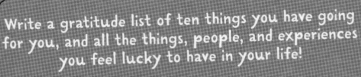

Write a gratitude list of ten things you have going for you, and all the things, people, and experiences you feel lucky to have in your life!

1. _____

2. _____

3. _____

4. _____

5. _____

6. _____

7. _____

8. _____

9. _____

10. _____

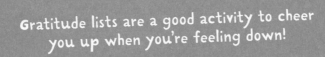

Gratitude lists are a good activity to cheer you up when you're feeling down!

1. _____

2. _____

3. _____

4. _____

5. _____

6. _____

7. _____

8. _____

9. _____

10. _____

Each of you grab a random book off a shelf, open it to a random page, pick a random word, and do a quick sketch of what that word means to you!

If they made a movie **about your life**,
which actor would you want to play your friend?

_____

_____

In the movie about your life, which **actor**
would you want to play you?

_____

_____

If they had to **rename your characters** in the
movie, what would you hope your name would be
changed to and what do you think your friend's
name should be changed to?

_____

_____

Write in the answers to the questions below.

Pick from the list below which describes you best.

I'm an early riser and I love the mornings!

I really hate getting up in the morning.

Neither, or maybe a little of both.

I don't know!

_____

_____

From the list below, choose which thing you do first when you get up in the morning.

Go to the bathroom, duh

Brush my teeth

Grab my phone

Eat something pronto

_____

_____

What's the **weirdest** thing you've ever put a **condiment** (for example, ketchup, mayonnaise, mustard, hot sauce) on?

_____

_____

What's the weirdest thing you've ever put **peanut butter** on?

_____

_____

What's the **strangest flavor combo** that actually tastes pretty darn good (like pickles and chocolate or French fries and milkshakes)?

_____

_____

What are your **top pet peeves** when it comes to making new friends? (For instance, maybe you can't stand someone who talks about themselves too much or someone who constantly interrupts.)

Who's your **fave family member**?
Why is that person your favorite?

_____

_____

_____

_____

If you could **trade one family member** for a
member of your BFF's family, who would you trade?
Why?

_____

_____

_____

_____

Do you consider yourself to be an
introvert or an **extrovert**?

_____

_____

What's your favorite thing to do **alone**?

_____

_____

What's your favorite thing to do with **other people**?

What do you think you would like? What do you think you would dislike? What do you think it would be like for you?

Draw pictures of each other's faces, then give each other majorly different hairstyles!

Ask your BFF to rate your new hairstyle!

Make a list of your top five
all-time **favorite love songs**,
and write who they make you
think of. Awww.

_____

_____

_____

_____

_____

_____

_____

_____

_____

If you could set up your best friend with anyone, living or dead, who would it be and why? King Tut? James Dean? Marilyn Monroe? Write down three candidates and explain why you think they'd be a great fit for your BFF. Be creative!

_____

_____

_____

_____

_____

Without thinking too hard about it, do a quick sketch of five things you'd give anything to eat or drink right this second!

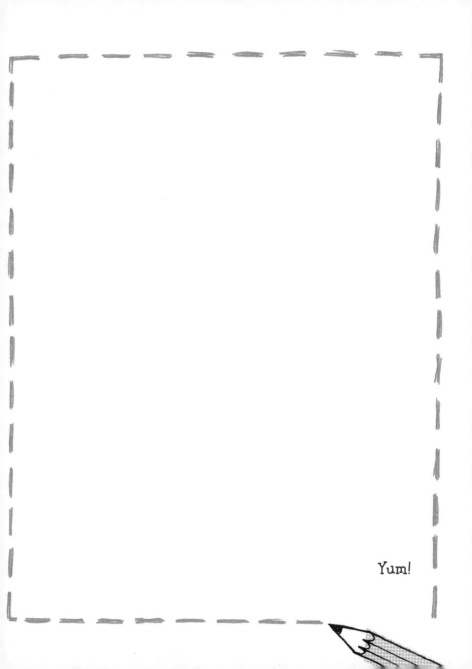

Yum!

What are your resolutions or goals for this year? Write down three things you want to accomplish in the next year and why they're important to you.

1. _____
   _____

2. _____
   _____

3. _____
   _____

1. _____
   _____

2. _____
   _____

3. _____
   _____

Write in the answers to the questions below.

If you could select your school's new mascot from any of the critters below, which would you choose?

Grasshopper
Raccoon
Elephant
Ferret

_____ _____

If you had to pick one of the following animals as your own personal mascot, which one would you choose?

Leopard
Bear
Hawk
Dolphin

_____ _____

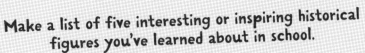

Make a list of five interesting or inspiring historical figures you've learned about in school.

1. _____   1. _____

2. _____   2. _____

3. _____   3. _____

4. _____   4. _____

5. _____   5. _____

Which of these figures would you most want to swap lives with for a month? Which would you be least likely to want to swap with?

_____

_____

_____

_____

If producers decided to make a **reality show** based on your school, what would you suggest the show be called?

_____

_____

Which particular **students** would you tell them to focus on, and why?

_____

_____

Would you want them to **film you and your BFF**? Why or why not?

_____

_____

_____

_____

On this page and the next, you and your BFF fill in the blanks. Then compare your answers!

When I'm in awkward situations where

I don't know what to talk about, I tend to

_____. I don't know if that's

_____, but it's what I do! The last

time I was in an _____

spot, I became very _____.

_____ was with me. I had to

_____! I eventually realized

_____ about myself.

When I'm in **awkward situations** where I don't know what to **talk** about, I tend to _____. I don't **know** if that's _____, but it's what I do! The last **time** I was in an _____ spot, I became very _____. _____ was with me. I had to _____! I **eventually** realized _____ _____ about myself.

Think up two facts and one lie **about yourself**. Tell them to your BFF, who has to **guess** which one is the lie. Now switch roles. For example, you might say "I had my first kiss at age twelve, I won the state track championship in high school, and I once went swimming with sharks."

Truth: _____

Truth: _____

Lie: _____

Truth: _____

Truth: _____

Lie: _____

Did your best bud know the truth from the lie?

_____

_____

Would you rather fall into a giant vat of poop **OR** puke?

_____

_____

Would you rather get food poisoning and
projectile-vomit twelve hours a day for a week straight
OR have diarrhea for a week straight?

_____

_____

Would you rather never fall in love **OR** fall in love once
but have a bad breakup with that person?

_____

_____

What do you imagine aliens look like?
Think closely about it!

Imagine an alien's face shape, eye color, eye shape, and mouth (or lack of a mouth) and then draw one!

If your BFF was a piece of **candy** or **chocolate**, which kind would your friend be? For example, "My BFF would be a Warhead because she's often sour and aggressive, but sweet underneath it all!"

_____

_____

If your BFF were a **beverage**, what kind would your friend be?

_____

_____

If your BFF were a snack food, what kind of **snack food** would your friend be?

_____

_____

What's your **favorite** kind of **exercise**? Why?

_____

_____

If you had to pick an exercise you could
never ever do again, which would you choose?

_____

_____

What's the **funniest thing** that's ever happened to
you while doing your favorite exercise?

_____

_____

_____

_____

Look outside the window and find a tree. Look at the tree closely for two minutes sharp (time yourself). Now doodle it quickly below without looking at it!

Make sure to inspect every inch of your tree to
get a detailed drawing of it.

Answer the questions below about your best friend.
Write the answer that fits your buddy best.

Of the choices below, the food my best friend likes the least is:

Brussels sprouts

Liver

Beef tongue

Lima beans

_____

_____

Of the choices below, the food my best friend would most want to eat is:

An ice cream sundae

Chips and salsa

A huge bucket of movie popcorn

A big bag of gummy candy

_____

_____

Come up with your own idea for a young adult (YA) **novel**!
Who's the **main character**?

_____

_____

What **happens** to him or her?

_____

_____

How would the book **end**?

_____

_____

_____

_____

Make a list of five things that get you out of bed every day. You can write deep, meaningful things, like your relationship with your parents.

1. _____

_____

2. _____

_____

3. _____

_____

4. _____

_____

5. _____

_____

You could also can list silly things,
like your enduring love of breakfast foods
or your awesome sticker collection!

1. _____

_____

2. _____

_____

3. _____

_____

4. _____

_____

5. _____

_____

Write a poem about jealousy.

What, to you, is the worst emotion
you could possibly feel?

What's the nicest thing your crush has ever said to or about you?

_____

_____

Who's the most bizarre person you've ever had a crush on?

_____

_____

If you and your crush went on a romantic dinner date, where would you want to go?

_____

_____

What are your feelings about **plaid**?

_____

_____

How do you feel about **school uniforms**?

_____

_____

Flip-flops: tacky or necessary?

_____

_____

Would you rather be forced to go to church every day for the rest of your life **OR** never go to a party again?

_____

_____

Would you rather eat glass shards **OR** walk on nails?

_____

_____

Would you rather lose the ability to speak
OR lose the ability to hear?

_____

_____

Write out some of the most **annoying aspects** of going to **school** every day. These could be things like "Homeroom is too cold" or "Mrs. Falton is mean." Be honest!

_____

_____

_____

_____

_____

_____

_____

_____

_____

Grab your favorite photo of you and your family (or with your BFF!) and draw a very careful copy of it.

Do your best to be faithful and make it look as much like the photo as possible!

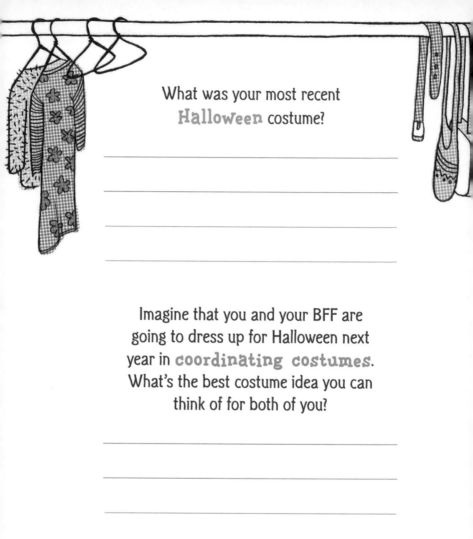

What was your most recent **Halloween** costume?

_____

_____

_____

_____

Imagine that you and your BFF are going to dress up for Halloween next year in **coordinating costumes**. What's the best costume idea you can think of for both of you?

_____

_____

_____

_____

Have you and your BFF ever
LIKE-liked the same person?

_____

_____

If so, what happened? Did you compete for
the person's attention or not so much?

_____

_____

If you've never liked the same
person, why do you think that is?

_____

_____

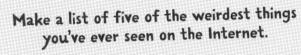

Make a list of five of the weirdest things you've ever seen on the Internet.

1. _____
2. _____
3. _____
4. _____
5. _____

1. _____
2. _____
3. _____
4. _____
5. _____

Now make a list of five of the greatest things you've ever seen on the Internet (for example, cat videos, men hugging lions, whatever!).

1. _____

2. _____

3. _____

4. _____

5. _____

1. _____

2. _____

3. _____

4. _____

5. _____

How do you feel about **classical music**?

_____

_____

Are there any **classical artists** or
songs that you like?

_____

_____

_____

_____

What does classical music make you
think about or **feel** when you listen to it?

_____

_____

_____

_____

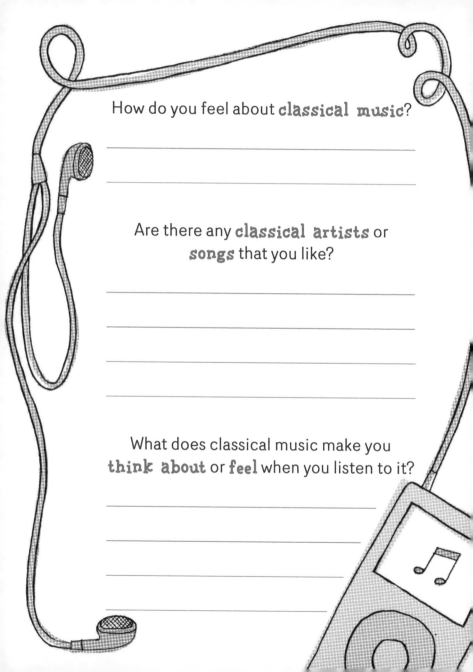

What's your **favorite thing to do** with your BFF?

_____

_____

_____

_____

How **often** do you get to do it?

_____

_____

_____

_____

What do you think **your BFF's favorite thing**
to do with you is?

_____

_____

Draw a special rendition of the worst Thanksgiving dish you ever had. EVER.

Yuck!

Make a list of five words that **described you** when you were seven years old.

1. _____   1. _____

2. _____   2. _____

3. _____   3. _____

4. _____   4. _____

5. _____   5. _____

Now create another list describing who you are **today**.

1. _____   1. _____

2. _____   2. _____

3. _____   3. _____

4. _____   4. _____

5. _____   5. _____

How have you **changed** (or not really changed) over time?

_____

_____

_____

_____

_____

_____

Are you surprised by how many things the current you
has in common with the younger you?

_____

_____

_____

_____

_____

What do you think would happen if all the adults in the world mysteriously evaporated and kids were suddenly forced to rule absolutely everything?

_____
_____
_____
_____
_____
_____
_____
_____
_____
_____
_____
_____
_____

Write out a paragraph about how you think things would change and how the kids would handle their newfound responsibility.

Write in the answers to the questions below.

If I had to choose from the names below, the name I'd choose to rename myself would be:

Cameron

Nico

Alden

North

_____   _____

If I had to choose from the names below, the name I'd be least likely to pick for myself would be:

Jaden

Axl

Luna

Ellsworth

_____   _____

Think about **your entire family**, and then pick **one word to describe** each family member. Write them all below! (Be sure to include the one word you'd use to describe your best friend!)

_____

_____

_____

_____

_____

_____

_____

_____

_____

On this page and the next, you and your BFF fill in the blanks. Then compare your answers!

I _____ reading! The last great

book I read was _____. When

I was younger, I _____ had

my face stuck in a book all the time. Reading

is _____ because

_____.

A book I've read and wish I'd written myself

is _____. If I could rewrite

it myself, I'd change _____

_____. The ending, to me,

was _____.

I _____ reading! The last great

book I read was _____. When

I was younger, I _____ had

my face stuck in a book all the time. Reading

is _____ because

_____.

A book I've read and wish I'd written myself

is _____. If I could rewrite

it myself, I'd change _____

_____. The ending, to

me, was _____.

Grab three small items off the bathroom shelf and doodle them below, just for the heck of it!

Did you and your BFF pick any of
the same items?

If you were going to start your very own **fashion magazine**, what would you name it?

_____

_____

What kinds of **features** would it include?

_____

_____

Think of a **story** idea you'd want to cover in your magazine and write it below.

_____

_____

_____

_____

What's your **favorite room** in your house? Why?

_____

_____

What's your **least favorite room**
in your house? Why?

_____

_____

What's your **favorite time of day**? Why?

_____

_____

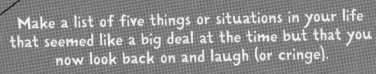

Make a list of five things or situations in your life that seemed like a big deal at the time but that you now look back on and laugh (or cringe).

1. _____

_____

2. _____

_____

3. _____

_____

4. _____

_____

5. _____

_____

How did you feel about them then, and how did your feelings about them change over time?

1. _____

_____

2. _____

_____

3. _____

_____

4. _____

_____

5. _____

_____

Would you rather go with your BFF on a luxury two-week tour of Europe by boat **OR** by train?

_____

_____

Would you rather win $50,000 in the lottery **OR** a dream car and dream apartment—with the condition that you wouldn't be able to move into the apartment or use the car until you were eighteen?

_____

_____

Would you rather develop a disease that made you sleep for twenty hours a day **OR** develop a disease that made your face incapable of showing emotion?

_____

_____

Write in the answers to the questions below.

Of the options below, what would you do if two of your best friends went to the movies without inviting you?

Not say anything, but silently sulk.

Yell at them both for leaving you out. The nerve!

Try really hard not to let them know you're bothered.

Cry about it all day.

_____

_____

From the list below, choose what you would do if your peanut-butter-and-jelly sandwich fell on the floor!

Leave it there and ask my mom to come pick it up.

Pick it up and throw it away, of course.

Pick it up, wipe it off, and eat it.

Pick it up and eat it without wiping it off. It's natural!

_____

_____

Write out a list of songs you'd put on a **playlist that had the theme** "Springtime Magical Fairy Convention."

_____   _____

_____   _____

_____   _____

_____   _____

_____   _____

_____   _____

_____   _____

_____   _____

_____

What do you hope to **accomplish** in your life?

_____

_____

_____

_____

Are you **afraid of death** or do you think it sounds like no big deal because it happens to everyone?

_____

_____

_____

_____

_____

Do you believe in love at first sight?
Why or why not?

_____

_____

Have you ever felt like you "loved"
someone (or just really, really liked
someone!) the very first moment you
laid eyes on them?

_____

_____

Who was it and what happened?

_____

_____

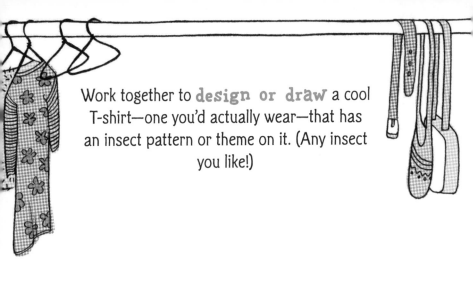

Work together to **design or draw** a cool T-shirt—one you'd actually wear—that has an insect pattern or theme on it. (Any insect you like!)

Where would you **wear it**?
Why did you choose the insect you did?

_____

_____

What's the **best advice** your BFF has ever given you?

_____

_____

What's the best **advice** you've ever
given your best friend?

_____

_____

What's the **worst advice** anyone has ever **given you**?

_____

_____

What's the most annoying excuse someone
can give to cancel plans?

_____

_____

How do you feel when someone cancels on you?

_____

_____

Have you ever skipped out on plans with a friend and
made him or her mad in the process?

_____

_____

If you designed a personal logo for your BFF, what would it look like?

For inspiration, think of a few of your favorite
logos for food joints, clothes, makeup, or whatever.

Make a list of things, people, and places that you associate with your number-one crush. For instance, if you met your love interest in line in the lunchroom, maybe you'd write "cafeteria." If you passed notes during math class, maybe you'd write "notes" or "math class." Be specific!

When's the last time you **took a risk**?

_____

_____

_____

_____

How did it **work out**?

_____

_____

_____

_____

Would you **do it again**?

_____

_____

On this page and the next, you and your BFF fill in the blanks. Then compare your answers!

When it comes to superstitions, I'm

_____. The superstition that gets

under my skin the most is _____.

I think it's funny when people believe in

_____, though.

_____ is something I used to

believe in when I was younger but totally don't

believe anymore.

_____ is something my friends

believe in but I don't.

When it comes to **superstitions**, I'm

_____. The superstition that gets

under my **skin** the most is _____.

I think it's funny when people **believe** in

_____, though.

_____ is **something** I used

to **believe** in when I was younger but totally

don't believe **anymore**.

_____ is something my

friends believe in but I don't.

What song can you just not get out of **your head** lately? Write the lyrics below.

_____

_____

_____

_____

_____

_____

_____

_____

_____

_____

_____

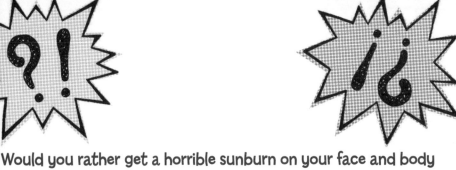

Would you rather get a horrible sunburn on your face and body and be forced to wear shorts and tank tops every day to show it off until it faded **OR** be afflicted with a condition that made you physically incapable of holding in your farts?

_____

_____

Would you rather live in a world without animals **OR** a world without trees?

_____

_____

Would you rather never be able to swim again **OR** never be able to dance again?

_____

_____

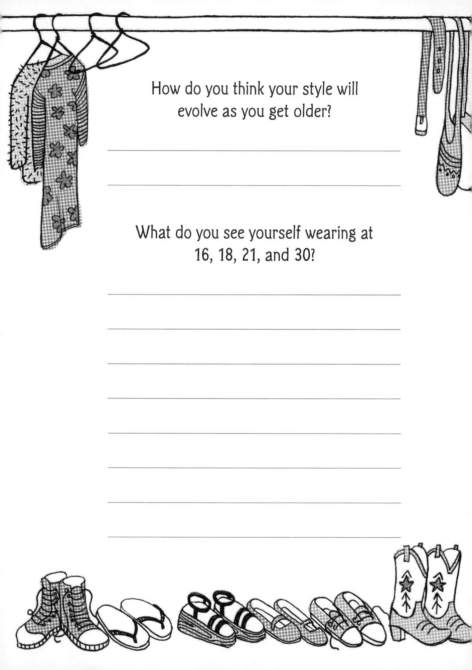

How do you think your style will evolve as you get older?

_____

_____

What do you see yourself wearing at 16, 18, 21, and 30?

_____

_____

_____

_____

_____

_____

_____

_____

Together, **pick a letter** of the alphabet. Then use that letter to come up with your own **tongue twister**, such as "Willa will willingly sell weeble wobbles while whistling wistfully!" Get together with your BFF and come up with three original tongue twisters. Then write them down below.

_____

_____

_____

_____

_____

_____

_____

Have your emotions ever gotten the best of you? (In other words, have you ever gotten totally overwhelmed with feelings about something?)

Write down a time you let your emotions
get the best of you and describe what happened.

If you could build a log cabin from scratch, what would it look like? Design your own log cabin and be sure to include lots of detail!

Is there a fireplace? How many rooms? Is it near a lake? Is there a fire pit outside for roasting marshmallows?

If you could date any character from a book, who would you want to date?

_____

_____

If you could date any character from a movie, who would you want to date?

_____

_____

If you could date any character from a TV show, who would you want to date?

_____

_____

Imagine you're driving away from a **scary hurricane** and you **see three people** at the bus stop: an old lady, your BFF, and your crush. You have room for only two extra people in the car! Write down **who you'd take** and why you chose them.

_____

_____

_____

_____

_____

_____

_____

_____

What's your **favorite time of day**?

_____

_____

Who's your **favorite artist**?

_____

_____

What's your **favorite holiday**?

_____

_____

Write down the ways that you and your BFF are **alike** and the ways that you're **different**.

_____

_____

_____

_____

_____

_____

How do you **deal** with your **differences**?

_____

_____

_____

_____

On this page and the next, you and your BFF fill in the blanks. Then compare your answers!

If I were **president** of the United States, the first

thing I would do is _____.

Another thing **I'd be sure to do** is _____

_____ and I **certainly** would never

forget to _____.

If my BFF were president, I **predict** the first

thing she'd **do** is _____

_____.

She would **probably** also _____

_____.

If I were **president** of the United States, the first

thing I would do is _____.

Another thing **I'd be sure to do** is _____

_____ and I **certainly** would never

forget to _____.

If my BFF were president, I **predict** the first

thing she'd **do** is _____

_____. She would

probably also _____

_____.

What musical instrument do you find the most
irritating or obnoxious to listen to?

_____

_____

Have you ever played that instrument yourself?

_____

_____

What do you do when you overhear someone playing
that instrument?

_____

_____

If you could go **back in time** and relive
the fashion from another era, what era would you
most like to dress in?

_____

_____

_____

_____

Describe a **dream outfit** that makes you
think of that particular time.

_____

_____

_____

_____

Imagine a world where there was no Internet, video games, and television. What would you do to pass the time?

_____

_____

_____

_____

_____

_____

_____

_____

_____

_____

_____

_____

_____

_____

_____

_____

How scary does that scenario seem to you?

Think back on the biggest fight you and your best friend ever had. Now sketch pictures of the way you think your faces must have looked during that fight—in the heat of the angriest moment ever!

Feel free to be funny and/or silly!

Would you rather be forced to drop out of school and be homeschooled by your parents **OR** not graduate from high school until you were twenty?

Would you rather drink a cup of goat's blood **OR** drink a cup of cat pee?

Would you rather never be able to eat bread again **OR** never be able to eat cheese again?

Write in the answers to the questions below.

Of the options below, which of these pastimes sounds most like something you'd want to take up?

Bobsledding

Car racing

Diving

Parasailing

_____   _____

Of the choices below, which of these activities sounds like the absolute opposite of fun to you?

Skiing

Running

Skydiving

High jumping

_____   _____

Do a quick sketch of something you ate last week (it should be something you loved!).

Tasty!

What's your biggest **irrational fear**?

_____

_____

Biggest **rational fear**?

_____

_____

What do you tell yourself when you're **feeling scared** about something? How do you talk yourself through it?

_____

_____

_____

_____

What are your **favorite toys** or **stuffed animals**, either from when you were younger or from more recently?

_____

_____

What **became of them** all?
Are they still in your house?

_____

_____

Have you ever **gotten rid of** a stuffed animal or toy and then totally **regretted it** later?

_____

_____

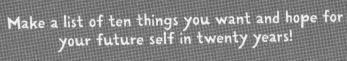

Make a list of ten things you want and hope for your future self in twenty years!

1. _____

2. _____

3. _____

4. _____

5. _____

6. _____

7. _____

8. _____

9. _____

10. _____

Be as detailed as you want to be. (For example, "Live in a spacious apartment in an old Victorian in San Francisco" or simply "Live in a cool city"!)

1. _____

2. _____

3. _____

4. _____

5. _____

6. _____

7. _____

8. _____

9. _____

10. _____

Music and emotions go together! Can you think of a time when music helped you **get through a rough time** in your life?

_____

_____

When was it? What happened? What were the songs or albums specifically that **helped you**?

_____

_____

_____

_____

_____

_____

Grab your BFF and put your heads together. Your task is to **create a dance** to one of your **favorite songs**! Then, if you're feeling bold, organize a recital of sorts and **perform your dance** routine for all your friends and family. You know you want to!

What song did you use for **your dance** routine?

On this page and the next, you and your BFF fill in the blanks. Then compare your answers!

For breakfast this **morning** I ate a nice big

portion of _____. I **drank** some

_____.

The best thing I **ate yesterday** was

_____, by far. The **best** thing

I **drank** was _____.

In general, my **fave meal** of the day is

_____ because _____

_____.

For breakfast this **morning** I ate a nice big

portion of _____. I **drank** some

_____.

The best thing I **ate yesterday** was

_____, by far. The **best** thing I

drank was _____.

In general, my **fave meal** of the day is

_____ because _____

_____.

What are your favorite **home-cooked meals**?

_____

_____

Who does most of the **cooking in your house**?

_____

_____

Do **you ever cook**?

_____

_____

Write in the answers to the questions below.

If you had to pick from the list below only one household appliance that you totally couldn't imagine living without, which one of these would it be?

Microwave

Alarm clock

Air conditioner

Refrigerator

_____   _____

If you had to pick from the list below one personal-grooming item you couldn't live without, which of these would you choose?

Hair dryer

Hair brush

Moisturizer

Lip balm

_____   _____

Make a list of five inventions that someone should seriously come up with, like yesterday. These inventions should improve your life in some way.

1. _____

2. _____

3. _____

4. _____

5. _____

1. _____

2. _____

3. _____

4. _____

5. _____

What's your style of flirting?
Are you subtle? Upfront? Shy?

_____

_____

Would you ever make the first move on
someone you liked?

_____

_____

Have you ever had a crush that was so
intense you almost couldn't bear to look
at the person? Who?

_____

_____

Do you ever think about where you might go to
high school?

_____

_____

How about where you might go to **college**?

_____

_____

Do **your parents** ever weigh in on
where they want you to go?

_____

_____

Pretend you're an inventor who just came up with a brand-new kind of **string instrument**. Describe it below. Be sure to explain both how it's played and what it's called!

_____

_____

_____

_____

Do you **play** any string instruments or any **instruments** at all?

_____

_____

_____

_____

Ask your BFF for a baby picture or another
cute childhood pic, then do your best
detailed drawing of that picture.

Awww. Cuties!

Would you rather get a disease that required you to inject yourself with shots once a day for the rest of your life **OR** have your life span cut short by five years?

Would you rather go swimming with sharks **OR** try bungee jumping?

Would you rather never see or speak to your crush ever again **OR** continue to be able to, BUT know that nothing would ever come of your feelings?

What would you do if you were **locked inside your favorite store** overnight?

_____

_____

What would you do if you were out to eat at a **fancy restaurant** but your soup came out with a cockroach floating in it?

_____

_____

What would you do if your BFF told you your **friendship** was dunzo?

_____

_____

_____

_____

Make a list of things you might do differently from your parents when, or if, YOU become a parent one day.

Do you think you want to have kids of your own someday?
Why or why not?

What's your favorite thing to do when you're **feeling super-crazy happy** and high on life?

_____

_____

What's your fave thing to do when you're **feeling dejected and down** in the dumps?

_____

_____

What about when you're **feeling angry**?

_____

_____

If you could choose one **person from history** to meet and chat with, who would you pick and why?

_____

_____

If you could choose one currently **famous person** to invite over for dinner, who would you ask and why?

_____

_____

If you met one of your **favorite celebs**, do you think you'd get starstruck? How would you deal?

_____

_____

_____

_____

On this page and the next, you and your BFF fill in the blanks. Then compare your answers!

The **worst fight** I ever got into was with

_____ about

_____.

When I'm in a fight with **someone**, I tend to

_____ but not

_____.

When I'm **making up with someone** after a fight,

I usually _____.

That **helps** me _____.

The **worst fight** I ever got into was with

_____ about

_____.

When I'm in a fight with **someone**, I tend to

_____ **but** not

_____.

When I'm **making up with someone** after

a fight, I usually _____.

That **helps** me _____.

Write about a time when you surprised yourself. Maybe you did better on a math test than you ever expected or maybe you broke out of your shy shell enough to play the lead in the school musical

Would you rather face off with a shark **OR** a leopard?

Would you rather have a pet ferret **OR** a pet fish?

Would you rather eat dirt **OR** drink a nice tall glass of
dirty bath water?

Whatever the case, write a description of what happened and how it made you feel. Does it make you feel proud?